Kevin-you're something special

says Jimmy Hill

playing the game itself (I am not referring to off-the-field endorsements). Secondly, he is the first rich footballer in those terms who is seen to dedicate himself entirely to his profession. Unlike some others, he is a perfect example for young people to look up to; he has good manners, is pleasant, even charming, and turns up when he is expected.

Keegan is a business man and his business is football. The main tool of his trade is his body. Part of the price that has to be paid for the kind of rewards he gets is that, single-mindedly, he must dedicate his life to keeping himself fit enough to produce the kind of extraordinary performance that is expected of a man of his calibre once or twice a week.

There is no doubt in my mind that Keegan has improved over 50 per cent since he has been playing for Hamburg. He is sharper, more aware tactically, and has the increased confidence to try anything, regardless of failure. A lot of that confidence has arisen from plenty of money in the bank, but there are other factors that have helped. Not least, the confidence which can be acquired by going into strange territory, learning another language and building a new life among different people. That has made Keegan—and would make anyone else, for that matter—a more mature player.

Keegan is always more than ready to dash back at the drop of a hat and play for England with maximum enthusiasm.

It is the enormous power that he packs into that very small frame that makes Kevin special. At times he jumps like a six-footer and resists tackles with the strength of Tommy Smith, but his low centre of gravity gives him such an advantage when it comes to turning an opponent and losing him in three electric strides; there is strength, agility and immediate acceleration tied up in one parcel and there are very few defenders in the world that can cope with that ebullient mix. Bertie Vogts found it in Munich, Romeo Benetti at Wembley.

Finally, it is to be observed that it is the very wideness of Kevin's appeal that is unique. A chap could take him home to tea and find that at the end of the day his wife, his mother, his teenage daughter and his au pair girl had all fallen under the spell of Keegan's charm. But, Kevin being Kevin, the chap wouldn't mind.

£1·50

My World Cup Dream

by Kevin Keegan

(talking to Brian Gearing)

I HAVE a dream—that in 1982 I will help England win the World Cup in Spain. Throughout my life I've thrived on challenges. I need ambition to drive me on. I need targets. And World Cup success for England in 1982 is the most important challenge of all . . . and the one I'm most determined to achieve.

I've been lucky as a player. Through playing with successful club sides I've won most of the honours at club level and I've been Footballer of the Year in Britain and European Footballer of the Year. But it's been a different story at international level. In my years as an England player, we've struggled.

Football, like everything else, goes in cycles. We were at the top in 1966, but you can't stay there for ever. I'll never forget the nightmare of England losing to West Germany in the 1970 World Cup in Mexico. I was watching the match on TV in a Doncaster pub. England led West Germany 2–0 at half-time, and I remember someone on the box saying

that there was now no way in which England could lose. We lost 3–2. That was the end for England and we've been fighting to find our way back ever since.

But we are believing in ourselves again. Playing for Ron Greenwood is a joy. He achieves just the right balance of being free and easy without being too free and easy—players are encouraged to go out there and play and to express their own ideas. For me, the thrill of playing for England is new every time I pull on my England shirt, and I'm sure the rest of the squad feel the same way.

My last game for Liverpool was in Rome—the night we beat Borussia Moenchengladbach to win the 1977 European Cup. The memory of that match will live with me forever. What a way to bow out! I had left Liverpool with the European Cup and the Football League Championship. If I can climax my England career with a similar success story, well, it *will* be a dream come true. I'll be 31 in 1982 and it would be unrealistic to expect to be around as a player for the next World Cup. So I'll be content to sign off as an England international after 1982. But as for retiring

Kevin Keegan on the attack for England . . . "For me, the thrill of playing is new every time I pull on my England shirt."

altogether, that's different. I love my football, and I intend to go on playing the game as long as I enjoy it.

My earliest football memories take me back to my home in the heart of Doncaster. Number 25, Spring Gardens was a Coronation Street-type terraced house, but it had a back garden—long and narrow with lilac bushes down one side and a big brick wall on the other. There was room for six or seven kids to kick the ball about and I remember that I always wanted to be Billy Wright, the Wolves and England captain. Our toilet was in the garden, and our games of football soon cost it its windows—shattered because our passes weren't always as accurate as they might have been.

My family is working class—my dad, Joe, was a Geordie miner who moved to Yorkshire when work was scarce on the Durham seams. I've got a sister, Mary, who is two years older than I am and a brother, Mike, who is seven years younger. Mum and Dad had tiffs, as all married people do, but I can't remember their having a serious argument. Dad liked his beer—which wasn't surprising considering the amount of time he spent under ground—and he liked a bet. But he was, in every sense of the word, a good man.

My Mum and Dad brought me up to respect correct standards of behaviour. Even today I find it difficult to call anyone older than myself by their first name. Manners, as they say, cost nothing, and yet they are a great thing. It's not hard to say please and thank you but today they are words that seem to be heard less and less. Take it from me, I'll sign my autograph for any youngster who says please; I might think twice if he doesn't.

Discipline, respect for other people and other people's feelings, correct behaviour— they all begin at home. You learn them among your family. Your teachers and the place where you work build on the foundations you've found at home. They can't do it on their own. Ask any teacher about the tearaways in their class and they'll point to a lack of proper guidance from the youngster's parents.

I had no problems in that direction—I wish my Dad, who died in 1976, was alive now to be having his beer and his bet and giving me the benefit of his good advice.

Hooliganism has been rife in British football and yet at Liverpool there has been very little rough stuff. For this, I credit Bill Shankly, the manager who took me to Liverpool and who was, genuinely, "the King

of the Kop". No manager ever had the kind of relationship with a crowd that Shanks had. The respect between Shanks and the fans made him more important to them than any single player. They prided themselves on their record of good behaviour. They did not want to let Shanks down. I've seen troublemakers taken to one side and given a good hiding by lads from the Kop. They'd try reasoning first but if that failed, the offender got a belting. Rough justice, certainly, but it proved more effective than any action taken by a policeman.

Having said that, I feel that football is to some extent carrying the can for what is really a social problem. Hooliganism is certainly the child of frustration—in the main it occurs at clubs starved of success or at clubs which slip after becoming used to a place among the élite.

I was a late starter as a footballer. At secondary school in Doncaster, nobody encouraged me—in fact, the sports master said I'd never make a professional. I got a trial for Doncaster Rovers but when I turned up no one was there. I then had a trial for Coventry City and was turned down. Guess

who the manager was? Jimmy Hill!

So at 16, armed with two O-Levels, I looked for a job and became a junior clerk in the store room of Peglers Brass Works, starting at £5 a week. Then—rescue! Scunthorpe United saw me playing for the Works reserve team and offered to take me on as an apprentice.

I started at Scunthorpe at £7, cleaned the lavatories, swept the terraces and ran the baths for the first team. It was at Scunthorpe that I took up weight training and managed to shoot up from 5ft to my present 5ft 7in. That's still on the small side, I know, but as Bill Shankly once said I'm "built like a tank", which accounts for the name the Hamburg fans shout when I appear on the field—"Mighty Mouse".

By 1971 I was 20 years old and a regular in Scunthorpe's first team. There were endless stories about big clubs watching me but nothing ever seemed to happen. As I've said, I need new challenges and I began to get depressed and frustrated. I even thought of quitting football and going back to Peglers.

Then in May 1971 Bill Shankly signed me

"My game is completely centred on my work rate. I get involved for the full 90 minutes . . ." Kevin Keegan in all-out action for (from left), Liverpool, England and the club he left Liverpool to join, the German side, Hamburg SV.

for Liverpool. The fee was £30,000 and I thought the most I could hope for was the odd first team game. But I was given my chance at the start of the next season and once I was in the first team there I stayed. In my six years with Liverpool I was lucky enough to be in the side that dominated English football and then Europe, too.

I try to be honest about my qualities as a footballer. I do not look upon myself as a skilful player. I know what I can and cannot do. If people use the expression "world class" I hope they do so because I know how to bring out the best in the players around me and therefore make a better player of myself. My game is completely centred on my work rate. I get involved for the full 90 minutes and receive the ball so much because I have an appetite for it.

It was my restless need for new challenges

Farewell to the Kop . . . it's May 14 1977 and Kevin Keegan plays his last game at Anfield. He helped Liverpool to a goal-less draw against West Ham.

that led me to leave Liverpool. Only my wife, Jean, knew how I felt. I tried as hard and trained as hard, but I felt my game had gone stale. I wasn't moving forward any more. I wasn't improving or developing as a footballer or as a person. I needed the adventure back again.

So at the end of the 1977 season, I moved to Hamburg SV. The fee was £500,000, a record for the Bundesliga. I don't think the Liverpool fans understood at first, but that's

changed with time. Funnily enough, I think I'm better liked in Britain now I've gone to play abroad.

I had a lot of problems at first. I realise now that anyone who changes countries and can't speak the language must expect problems. You can't communicate, it's as simple as that. It's certainly a problem I underestimated. At home, if I felt someone was a bit off me for any reason I'd just go up and ask them what was wrong. I couldn't do that in Germany. I had to bottle it up.

I couldn't help recalling how some British footballers—Jimmy Greaves and Denis Law among them—had tried playing for foreign clubs and then returned home disappointed by the experience. I told myself that there was no way I was going to do that. But if some other foreign club had come after me, I think I would have gone.

Things improved as my German got better —but the best thing that happened was the arrival of Gunther Netzer, the German World Cup star. He joined Hamburg as the new manager and laid down in training that from then on the style of play was to feed me. His point was that you either play to the strengths of someone like me—or sell them. I can tell you, it was like the sun rising.

I've been forced to develop my game— firstly, because things went wrong at the start, and, secondly, because of the nature of the German game itself. In England, games are won or lost in the midfield. In Germany, the midfield is surrendered. They keep a spare man, the libero, at the back but everyone else marks man to man. It means, if you beat a man, you can have a 60–70 yard run in empty space before you reach the next opponent. I don't have to wheel round the way I did in England, looking for space.

Are the Germans more skilful than British footballers? It's difficult to answer that one. The real point, I feel, is that with Liverpool I used to average 60 to 70 games a season. In Germany, because there are fewer teams in the Bundesliga than there are in the English First Division and because there are fewer competitions, the most competitive games I'll play is about 40. So in Germany we spend more of our time training instead of actually playing and the coach has the opportunity to develop the players' skills.

For me, one thing about football in Germany is exactly the same as it was with Liverpool. Just before the kick-off, I always eat a bar of chocolate. I'm convinced it gives me energy, and the way I play I need it! Steak, for example, takes 24 hours to digest whereas chocolate gets to work on you within an hour.

For me to play a game without having eaten my bar of chocolate is unthinkable. I need the chocolate as much as I need a new challenge. I'll make sure I'll have a good supply with me for Spain 1982!

Win a day out with Kevin Keegan

EVERY YOUNGSTER wants to meet his sporting hero—and there's no greater hero in sport today than Kevin Keegan.

Match of the Day annual offers you the chance to spend a day in Hamburg with Kevin, all expenses paid. He'll take you to a football match—who knows, he might even be playing in it!—make sure you're shown round the city and join you for a meal.

To win this exciting day out, you must answer correctly the six questions listed below and then say, in not more than 25 words, why you would like to spend a day with Kevin Keegan. There will also be six runners-up who will each receive a football specially autographed by Kevin. The winner and runners-up will be chosen by Kevin Keegan, Jimmy Hill and the editor of Match of the Day. The name of the winner will be announced on Match of the Day during March 1980. The runners-up will be notified by post. The decision is final and binding and no correspondence will be entered into.

To enter our competition you must be 16 years old or younger. You may only enter once. You must not work for the BBC or be related to anyone employed by the BBC. The competition is open only to residents of the United Kingdom and the Republic of Ireland. On your day out with Kevin Keegan you will be accompanied by a BBC representative. Closing date is January 31 1980.

Now for the six questions:

A. **Many famous goalkeepers have played for England—which one has won the most caps?**
B. **Who has scored the most goals for Scotland in official internationals?**
C. **Who is N. Ireland's most capped player?**
D. **When did England play their first official international?**
E. **Who took over from Alf Ramsey as the man in charge of the England team?**
F. **Who is the only player to collect FA Cup-winners' medals at Wembley in two successive seasons playing for different clubs?**

List your answers on a postcard and write your words about Kevin Keegan, beginning with the phrase: **I would like to spend a day with Kevin Keegan because** . . . Add your name, age and address and then post to: Kevin Keegan Competition, Room G.075, BBC Kensington House, Richmond Way, Shepherd's Bush, London W14 0AX.

Match of the Day first appeared on your BBCtv screens in 1964—and it was soon covering the build-up to England's 1966 World Cup triumph. On these two pages: six players from the side that beat West Germany at Wembley in that dramatic and never-to-be-forgotten final.

GORDON BANKS' career at top level was prematurely ended by an eye injury. He began with Leicester City and later played for Stoke City. He was England's goalkeeper in the 1966 and 1970 World Cup competitions and justifiably rated as the world's number one at the height of a career which brought him 73 international appearances.

BOBBY MOORE holds the record as England's most-capped player—he made 108 appearances. He started his England career in 1962 and played until 1973. He spent most of his playing life with West Ham United making a record 544 League appearances there before moving to Fulham in March 1974. He was an outstanding defender and England captain.

BOBBY CHARLTON holds three records for Manchester United—he made 606 League appearances and scored 198 goals as well as being their most capped player with 106 full England appearances. He played for them between 1956 and 1973. He scored more goals than any other England player, reaching 49, and was outstanding in 1966.

GEOFF HURST is the only player to score a hat-trick in a World Cup Final—and he did it against West Germany in 1966. He made over 400 League appearances for West Ham United, scoring 180 goals, before finishing his League career with Stoke City. Later he became assistant to England's Ron Greenwood and Chelsea's coach.

HALL OF FAME · HALL OF FAME · HALL OF FAME · HALL OF FAME · HALL OF FAME ·

ALAN BALL, an effervescent midfield player, reached his 600th League appearance in the 1978–79 season in a career which has embraced Blackpool, Everton, Arsenal and Southampton. His international career produced 72 caps for England over a ten-year period.

MARTIN PETERS, a midfield maestro, completed his 600th League appearance in the 1977–78 season. He started his career with West Ham United, making his debut at 18 in April 1962. His subsequent career has taken him to Tottenham Hotspur and Norwich City. He made 67 full appearances for England.

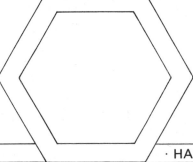

· HALL OF FAME ·   HALL OF FAME ·

PAT JENNINGS, Northern Ireland's most capped player, made his 80th international appearance against Denmark in June 1979. A goalkeeper of genuine world class, he started in his native country with Newry and came to England to join Watford. Transferred to Tottenham Hotspur in June 1964, he set up a club record there in making 472 League outings for them. He was the subject of another move across the North London area when he signed for Arsenal in time for the 1977–78 season. He has been a consistent choice at club and international level since his early emergence.

· HALL OF FAME · HALL OF FAME · HALL OF FAME · HALL OF FAME ·

VIV ANDERSON. When he was selected to play for England against Czechoslovakia in November 1978 Viv Anderson became the first coloured player to represent England at senior level. A right-back, he had previously been capped at Under-21 level. Originally with Nottingham Forest as an apprentice, he signed professional forms at the start of the 1974–75 season and made his League debut during the same campaign. He helped Forest back to the First Division and won League championship honours with them in 1977–78. His second cap was against Sweden in June 1979.

HALL OF FAME · HALL OF FAME · HALL OF FAME · HALL OF FAME ·

Football's future...

Jimmy Hill takes a glimpse into the 80s

I DON'T PRETEND to be a fortune teller and certainly not a gypsy—but I am prepared to try my hand and predict the way football will progress in the eighties.

There are three ways to look ahead. The first, to imagine things that almost certainly will happen; then to imagine things that might well happen; and, perhaps the most enjoyable of all, although it can lead to a fair amount of frustration, to wish for all the things that one would like to see happen.

Football officials are a conservative bunch and, as a result, the game has changed very slowly through the years. Its legislators are not renowned for making electric decisions; they prefer to wait for changes to occur in the natural course of evolution. So I am not predicting revolutionary happenings.

One thing I am absolutely certain about is that football, rightly called the world game, really will become the world game In the 1980s. Measuring the World Cup television audiences through the years gives some indication of what will happen.

For instance, the 1966 World Cup was watched by a television audience of about 250 million. By 1974 it had crept up to just over 400 million and in 1978 was estimated at around the 500 million mark. But, with the interest in soccer growing apace in the United States (incidentally, where the World Cup is yet to be televised) another 100 million could soon be added to that audience.

In Africa, the Middle East, the Far East, and to a lesser extent in Canada, Australia and South Africa, the enthusiasm for football is catching on faster than a bush fire.

In the past year I have seen the Chinese and Koreans play an exuberant game. Their attitude to the game is quite refreshing— professionals in this country might call it

Will we ever see this at our grounds?
In America they show action highlights
for the fans at the match.

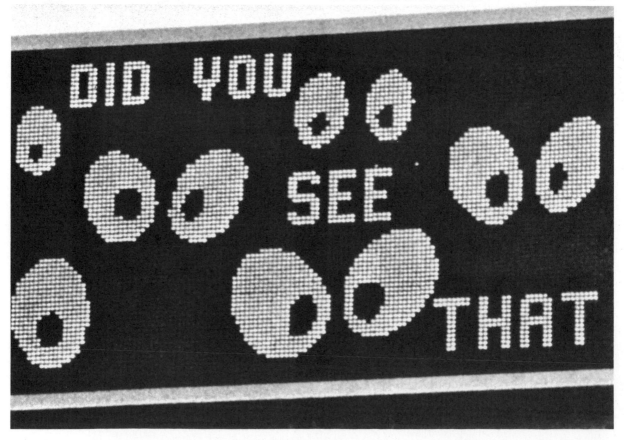

The exuberant Koreans . . . they delight in the skills of football and defeat still doesn't sour their enjoyment.

naive—but it is pleasing to see the way they delight in performing the skills and haven't yet reached the stage where a loss takes away their pleasure.

The Arabs, too, are on the way to making a tangible contribution. They are not yet all blessed with adequate facilities or the right kind of climate throughout the year to stimulate progress. They are quick, nimble and have a fine feel and touch for the ball, but they'll have to add consistency and discipline to their natural ability before they reach the targets they seek so enthusiastically.

When the Americans really get to grips with the game they could provide the most fascinating contribution of the lot. Their basic problem at the moment is a desperate shortage of coaches at lower levels.

We don't realise how lucky we are in this country that fathers can teach sons the simple skills. It's the kind of knowledge that has been passed on from generation to generation since the game started in the 19th century.

Three things might rub off from America at some stage in the future. They are: summer football, astroturf and full-size football pitches indoors. Quite honestly I can't see any of them happening here before 1990 for a variety of reasons.

With summer football I don't think anybody could be absolutely certain that it would improve crowds.

As to astroturf, it's produced some very presentable and entertaining games in the United States but I don't think I would like to see League football played entirely on that surface in this country. It's too predictable and there's nothing like a good slippery, muddy ground for entertainment. Defenders make mistakes in the mud . . .

I can't honestly see sufficient clubs having the capital to build astrodomes here so that the game can be played indoors. There isn't one club with the money to do it.

I do expect more clubs to find ways of avoiding postponement of matches from frost, ice and snow. At Coventry City we have recently introduced a form of under-soil heating, which we hope will be successful and spread. Hot water is passed through plastic piping—21 miles of it—which should keep the ground soft under any extreme conditions.

Nothing is more annoying for spectators and expensive, too, than the late cancellation of a game due to bad weather.

While we are on the subject of fans, let's take a moment to look at the facilities that should be there by the end of the 80s.

I am sure by that time nearly everybody will be seated at the major grounds in this country. Apart from any other consideration it's the best answer to hooliganism on the basis that it's much harder to be a hooligan sitting down.

In America the paying customer comes first . . . everyone gets a seat and a wealth of facilities are provided.

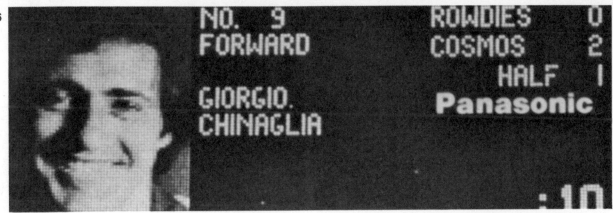

NO. 9
FORWARD

GIORGIO.
CHINAGLIA

ROWDIES 0
COSMOS 2
HALF 1
Panasonic

:10

The huge electronic scoreboard lights up to spell out the latest situation . . . another aspect of soccer, USA-style.

I can see clubs providing more and more facilities for the up-market supporter and less and less for those who have proved a nuisance to them over the years.

There will be no shortage of applicants for any luxury facilities that a football club provides. I can see clubs moving towards a system where their supporters become members of the club itself, enjoying a variety of sports facilities provided for them.

However luxurious the facilities on offer, few people want them without the accompanying advantage of a car park space and that's a problem for many clubs. There just isn't the land available immediately adjacent to their grounds, because they are nearly all in crowded areas. I don't see many of them having the opportunity or the money to move their ground to more spacious locations, but a regular bus ferrying service or even a car jockey service for privileged customers prepared to pay for it might be one way of dealing with this tricky problem.

It wouldn't be bad, would it? A spectator could drive his car to the appropriate entrance and let somebody whisk it off to the car park. With the match over, he could have a relaxing drink in the bar and check his pools coupon while waiting for his car to be returned to him.

In America they televise almost every match on closed circuit TV and many of the grounds have screens on which goals can be played back instantly. They are able to afford such luxury because there is a better return on the immense capital investment needed as a result of the wide variety of events that take place at those stadia. I can't see any football club in this country risking the necessary capital to launch such a project before 1990, but it's a target worth contemplating.

Now to the game itself. I would like to see changes made to the laws of the game that would make football more enjoyable for players and spectators. Why shouldn't we all try to get the maximum fun out of it?

Take the change of law in relation to the goalkeeper being in possession of the ball. That came about because goalkeepers went through a monotonous routine of rolling the ball, picking it up, bouncing it, walking with it, and generally taking their time before getting the ball back into play. But the law change did not work, and I would be delighted to see it adjusted so that a goalkeeper was not allowed to freeze the ball in the aggravating way it happens at the moment. That grotesque routine would be avoided if forwards were obliged to move away from the goalkeeper once he'd got the ball in his hands.

I would like to see the rest of the world take a good look at the American 35-yard line system. For me it takes away none of the traditional elements of the game, but does mean that there is more space in midfield for creative football to take place. There would be far less playground football—20 players locked round the ball with no room to swing a cat. How can players demonstrate their artistry in such crowded areas?

At the moment we see so much of what I call "hot potato" football with nobody having time to change the pace. Defensive players (which sometimes means ten) pressurise players in possession to such an extent that it suppresses thoughtful creativity.

The 35-yard line law is a simple and effective antidote. It operates so that, instead of it being possible for players to be off-side as soon as they are in their opponents' half, they can only be in an off-side position when they cross a line 35 yards from their opponents' goal. Thus when their team is attacking, defenders do not move up to the half-way line as happens conventionally and condense the play into one half of the field. They remain on their own 35-yard line to mark attackers lurking there. It's amazing how much this law changes the game for the better.

Surely in the 80s FIFA will tidy up one of the anomalies which I know aggravates many people. It's when a goalkeeper takes a short goal kick and the player he is passing to, finding himself pressurised by an attacker, moves into the 18-yard area and plays the ball before it gets out of the area. As the law stands the goalkeeper then gets another chance to take the kick, which is anomalous and not in keeping with the spirit of the other laws of the game in that there is no second chance.

I can't talk about the future without talking about my hobby-horse with regard to the ''second degree penalty''. I have thought about this for many years now and have reached the conclusion that it is the most beneficial change that could be made to the laws of the game. Simply, the law as I would propose it would give the referee power to award a direct free-kick—on the lines of a penalty—from the centre of the 18-yard area for acts of violence, ie professional fouls, punching, any cynical act that takes place outside the penalty area.

In this way all those abuses would become unprofessional, for by committing them a player could affect the score. I estimate that players would score perhaps one goal in two attempts from 18 yards, so that kind of violence would soon become unprofitable. Once again it would give skill and ability a chance to flourish.

How about the referee of the future? A lot of people are suggesting—and it has been tried in Germany—that the referee should have the advantage of watching television slow-motion replays before making key decisions in matches. Well, once again, because of expense, I don't see clubs being able to afford to provide that luxury for the officials, even if they wanted to.

I believe, as do the traditionalists, that the referee's word has to be final and has to be accepted even when he has made a mistake. The game is played not only at professional level in stadia throughout the world but by millions of lesser players, who may get as much, if not more, enjoyment from the game. Their games can be refereed only as they have been refereed since football started. The referee's decision has to be final.

There is one change I would like to see for linesmen, if not referees. In the depths of winter in this country there is nothing for me

more stupid than to see a linesman standing shivering in brief shorts. I am quite sure that cold affects their efficiency. I would give them gloves, even ear muffs if the weather is bad enough, and certainly tracksuit bottoms. They would still be able to cover the necessary ground and, at the same time, they would be more comfortable, relaxed and accurate.

Most of all in the 1980s I'd like to see fun back in the game. It has become such an obsession to win in far too many countries and leagues that the original object of the game of football has been completely forgotten. That object, as I have always seen it, is to enjoy an hour and a half of marvellous athletic exercise where the brain as well as the lungs and the legs gets its fair share of work, where flair and discipline, strength, speed, agility, determination, courage and aptitude are all put into the marvellous melting pot known as a game of football.

We must never forget the spirit of football, which for me is exemplified not so much by world stars winning World Cup competitions, nor yet legendary players stirring our memories. It's more about the pleasure that a young boy gets in rushing out on to the nearest piece of grass with a new pair of football boots or a new ball on Christmas morning. The fun he gets is the fun we should all continue to seek from this extraordinarily satisfying game.

Ardiles-soccer's

welcome stranger

by David Coleman

A WHOLE NEW era in English football began when Tottenham paid £750,000 for two Argentinians in the summer of 1978, but if ever one player deserved to write the first chapter of success it is Osvaldo Ardiles.

There's not much of Ardiles, who stands 5 feet 6 inches tall and weighs less than 10 stone. But what there is of the dainty little South American has already made a significant impact on English football in general and his new club in particular.

There were those who said that Tottenham were taking an outrageous gamble by inviting Ardiles and Ricardo Villa to exchange Argentinian football for the competitive and unfamiliar Football League, widely regarded as the hardest in the world. But their gamble has been more than justified, especially by the smaller, more talented player bought to reinforce a team that had scrambled into the First Division the season before in third promotion place.

The first of the foreign players to join English clubs, Ardiles and Villa were willing pioneers in a new adventure that, in Tottenham's case at least, soon paid off as huge crowds flocked in everywhere to watch them.

The formidable figure of Villa was makeweight in the deal so it was as expected that the slighter Ardiles influenced Tottenham's football, overcoming both his and the team's inevitable problems to play a major role in the consolidation of a side that might otherwise have been in serious trouble.

It was in June 1977 that Ardiles first really caught the attentions of an Englishman— Don Revie, then national team manager. During his penultimate game in charge of England, Revie turned to Ray Kennedy sitting on the substitute's bench to say: ''That number 4's a great player.''

Not long after that 1–1 draw in Buenos Aires, Revie left England for the United Arab Emirates and it was another year before Ardiles came under the fascinated scrutiny of Englishmen and the world at large again when his country staged the 1978 World Cup.

Ardiles stands only 5 feet 6 inches and weighs less than 10 stone, but, as he says, there's more to football than muscles.

Regarded as the best right-sided midfield player in the tournament by Revie's successor, Ron Greenwood, Ardiles enhanced even his own considerable reputation by helping Argentina to win the trophy for the first time. But his stay in his native land was to be limited.

Arsenal could have signed Ardiles when their manager, Terry Neill, was tipped off that he was available by Sheffield United's manager, Harry Haslam, on his return from Argentina. But Neill already had enough quality midfield players on his books and in turn he presented his ex-assistant at Tottenham, Keith Burkinshaw, with an opportunity he was not slow to grasp.

In best cloak-and-dagger tradition, Burkinshaw cleverly concealed his movements. He boarded a plane for South America—and the next thing the world knew, Ardiles and Villa were set to become Spurs players. The combined fee being dangled by Tottenham was small by present-day standards but, with Ardiles and Villa keen to receive what they were worth away from their own inflation-

racked country, the deal was settled in a remarkably short time.

Ardiles' club Huracan from Buenos Aires must have been particularly loath to lose such an outstanding performer but an astute mind had helped the little maestro establish himself on the field and he was not slow to appreciate—and accept—the opportunities being offered.

Brought up in the small town of Cordoba, where he had attended the university and law school for four years, Ardiles came to England not only to join a new club but also in the knowledge that he could complete his law studies for examinations in the summer of 1979. An academic among working-class footballers, Ardiles swiftly impressed his flair, intelligence and abundant skill on his new team-mates, who admittedly took their time adjusting to

Ardiles has a rich variety of football skills . . . he is a master of the flicked pass, a shrewd user of space and his balance keeps him on his feet where others stumble.

the qualities of the newcomer.

The master of the flicked pass, short sinuous dribble and a shrewd user of space, Ardiles also showed himself to be the possessor of tremendous balance that frequently enabled him to stay upright where others would stumble. He quickly settled down in the First Division even if Tottenham did not.

For a side that struggled at first, Tottenham attracted astonishingly big gates on their visits to the provinces and elsewhere, all of them curious, no doubt, to observe what the darting Ardiles had to offer.

The crowds may have marvelled at his ability, but the English defender has never been known to respect reputations and Ardiles soon discovered that he had to survive heavy, at times even savage, tackles.

He also had to survive the embarrassment of Spurs being crushed 7–0 at Liverpool in one of the season's early games.

It was as his first season drew to a close that Ardiles admitted that certain people had tried to kick him but he added that they hadn't impressed him because footballers' strengths were not measured by the size of their muscles. Nor did he believe there were many assassins in the English game, which he said had a better spirit than any he had encountered elsewhere. He observed that football in England was, in the main, played by gentlemen.

But there were some bad moments for Ardiles, not least the disappointment of failing to become the Players' "Player of the Year" after so much speculation that he would win the award from his fellow professionals. He had to be content with third place.

And with Tottenham failing to achieve any degree of consistency, Ardiles found himself shifted from midfield to the attack and back, as Burkinshaw desperately shuffled his players in an attempt to find a successful formula.

It didn't work since Ardiles lacked the weight and height of his compatriot Villa to be much of a threat up front, and in the League he failed to add to the three goals he scored from his favourite midfield position.

After he had overcome the extreme conditions of bone-hard pitches, snow, slush, mud and cold to perform brilliantly in the worst English winter for 16 years, the strain at last took its toll. Towards the end of the season, he was dropped for four games before returning with his appetite and enthusiasm renewed.

Ardiles knows now more of what is expected. Burkinshaw rammed home the message by omitting him, and Ardiles, who has been heard to say that no footballer works as hard as the English one, has spent his summer back in Argentina not only preparing for his examinations but ruminating over such English expressions as work rate. With his gifts it's certain that he's returned to Tottenham an even better equipped player than he was in his debut season.

Ardiles has been a marvellous ambassador for his country and we can all look forward to the further enjoyment his skills will bring to the First Division.

In his first season in Britain, Ardiles' skills defied the worst winter for 16 years.

FUNSPOT - FUNSPOT - FUNSPOT

If you want to make up your own fixture list for table top soccer games, five a side matches or even full team matches, here is an example of the formula you need to ensure every team plays each other twice and no more!

PLAN FOR EIGHT CLUBS

| Club: | 1 | 2 | 3 | 4 | 5 | 6 | 7 | 8 |
Match	v.	v.	v.	v.	v.	v.	v.	v.
1st	2	1	7	6	8	4	3	5
2nd	3	8	1	7	6	5	4	2
3rd	4	3	2	1	7	8	5	6
4th	5	4	8	2	1	7	6	3
5th	6	5	4	3	2	1	8	7
6th	7	6	5	8	3	2	1	4
7th	8	7	6	5	4	3	2	1
8th	8	7	6	5	4	3	2	1
9th	2	1	7	6	8	4	3	5
10th	3	8	1	7	6	5	4	2
11th	4	3	2	1	7	8	5	6
12th	5	4	8	2	1	7	6	3
13th	6	5	4	3	2	1	8	7
14th	7	6	5	8	3	2	1	4

Black Figures: Home Games
Red Figures: Away Games

With this plan for eight teams you can easily see how it can be adapted to suit whatever number of teams might meet your own requirements.

MICK MILLS captained Ipswich Town when they won the FA Cup in 1978 and he has been with the club as a professional since February 1966. He joined them after playing as a youth with Portsmouth and became an apprentice. Versatile enough to play either full-back or midfield, he has set up a new League appearance record for the East Anglian side, overhauling Tom Parker's 428 matches shortly after the start of the 1978–79 season. He made his 26th appearance for England against Austria in June 1979 and previously won honours at Under-23 level.

· HALL OF FAME · HALL OF FAME · HALL OF FAME · HALL OF FAME

PHIL PARKES became the most expensive goalkeeper in the world when West Ham United signed him from Queen's Park Rangers for a fee of £565,000 in February 1979. He started his career outside the League with Brierley Hill and joined Walsall where he made his Football League debut. Transferred to Queen's Park Rangers in May 1970 for £15,000, he later won England Under-23 honours and a full cap against Portugal in 1974. One of the tallest goalkeepers at around 6ft. 3in. and well built, he has completed a career total of more than 400 League appearances.

HALL OF FAME · HALL OF FAME · HALL OF FAME · HALL OF FAME ·

KENNY SANSOM, a talented left-back, made his 100th
League appearance for Crystal Palace early in the 1978–79 season.
Introduced for his League debut at the end of the 1974–75 season
against Tranmere Rovers, he made half a dozen more appearances
the following season before establishing himself in the team that
won promotion from the Third Division in 1976–77. Sansom, a
youth international, has since added England honours at Under-21
and full level with his attacking style of play. He is regarded
as a player who will feature regularly on the international scene.

· HALL OF FAME · HALL OF FAME · HALL OF FAME · HALL OF FAME ·

STEVE COPPELL was transferred to Manchester United from Tranmere Rovers in February 1975 for £50,000 after the Merseyside club had introduced him to League football the previous year. A forward who can play on the right flank or operate as a midfield player, he has a fine turn of speed. He gained an Economic History degree at Liverpool University and has won honours for England at Under-23 and full level, winning his 16th full appearance against Austria in June 1979. He played a key role in Manchester United reaching their third FA Cup final in four seasons.

HALL OF FAME · HALL OF FAME · HALL OF FAME · HALL OF FAME ·

England's man... a player's man -that's Ron Greenwood

says John Motson

THERE were two moments in his first year as England manager that convinced me Ron Greenwood was the man for the job. But neither took place anywhere near Wembley.

In fact, one was thousands of feet up in the sky, and the other was below ground level. But both served to illustrate that Greenwood is a man of many parts and not just a man for all football seasons.

We were some 6000 miles away from home, flying across Argentina from one World Cup city to another, when he first unfolded to me his philosophy on how the biggest job in English football should be tackled.

"What we have lacked up to now is a base. A foundation on which to build the sort of continuity our football needs from top to bottom. Too many different levels in our game are out of step with each other."

The fact that England were absent from the World Cup we were watching—and for the second time running at that—merely emphasised that a lot had gone wrong with English football since we were World Champions in 1966.

Greenwood continued: "A few years ago, the public got what they deserved. It did not matter how you won, as long as you won. The ball players were destroyed by people kicking them."

It was that type of physical approach Greenwood always abhorred as manager of West Ham. He went to the other extreme, encouraging a purist's approach which often

Ron Greenwood believes in telling his England players to go forward and improvise rather than fall back and worry.

cost him results but kept him his principles.

So it was no surprise in Argentina to hear Greenwood enthuse most about what the Europeans and South Americans could do with the ball. How they varied their attacks by clever positioning and intelligent running.

The Odeon Cinema in Leicester Square is a long way from the River Plate Stadium in Buenos Aires, but Greenwood made the two seem just next door when I witnessed the second little episode several months later.

On a bleak morning in our worst winter for years, with garbage piled high in London's streets during a refuse collectors' strike, Greenwood lifted the morale of a packed auditorium with more soccer sense.

His audience was 500 noisy schoolboys who were guests of the Football Association at a three-day teach-in. The address from the England manager, followed by question time, was the highlight of their trip.

Greenwood stressed the need for youngsters to learn how to *play* before they are taught how to compete. Developing their skills, and learning the fundamentals, should come before worrying about winning cups and medals.

Here was the base of the pyramid Greenwood was talking about on the aeroplane. He knows that what happens in schools today governs the type of footballer we get tomorrow.

Over the past 20 years, the transition from schoolboy star to accomplished professional has been fraught with pitfalls. And Greenwood does not entirely blame the schoolmasters.

"Apprentice professionals would appreciate how good a life a footballer has if they were sent out to work for two years before joining a football club. If they knew what it was like to work from nine to five, it would make them

Ron Greenwood brought in former England star Geoff Hurst (right) as one of his changes in the management structure.

more determined to do well in football''.

He believes the present system, where clubs take boys straight from school at 15, produces players who know no other side to life and rarely have to think for themselves.

It is this wide concern for the image of our national game, and for the welfare of those coming into it, that has stamped Greenwood as more than just a football manager.

His predecessors, Don Revie and Alf Ramsey, were arch-professionals who kept their ambitions centred very firmly on the full England team. Neither wavered in his belief that the most important priority was the result of the next international.

Greenwood saw the job rather differently. He got the fear of being judged on results out of his system a long time ago. He saw a way of winning in the long term, not just in the short term.

It was to give the international set-up a continuity that he restructured the management of all the England sides. Bill Taylor and Geoff Hurst were to be his assistants at senior level, Bobby Robson and Don Howe took charge of the 'B' team, Dave Sexton and Terry Venables assumed control of the Under-21s.

Some felt this coaching team was unwieldy. But Greenwood saw it as a co-operative society, with the best brains in English football making a valid contribution within a common policy.

Greenwood, after all, was once manager of the England Youth team. After that, the Under-23s. But although his appointment as overall leader may appear logical in those terms, it came completely out of the blue.

He admits: ''Towards the end of my time at West Ham, the cynical attitude in the game made me very disillusioned. I moved down to the South Coast to prepare for retirement''.

But cometh the hour, cometh the man. In the wake of Don Revie's clouded departure, England needed a sort of high priest. In the words of FA chairman, Sir Harold Thompson: ''We were looking for complete integrity''.

On the day Greenwood was appointed, following a few months as caretaker manager, Thompson spoke of the new man's "intelligence and knowledge at all levels of football".

Greenwood replied: "It is my job to pick players who will make England successful, playing the way we believe England should be represented".

The teams he has picked since reflect those sentiments entirely. Suddenly, after a period of pessimism and instability, there was a smile back on the face of the England team.

The introduction of wingers like Steve Coppell and Peter Barnes; the selection of attacking midfield players like Tony Currie and Trevor Brooking; the encouragement to go forward and improvise rather than to fall back and worry. All this stimulated the England players.

Greenwood had believed in attacking on a broad front since his early coaching days at Arsenal. It was a philosophy that made West Ham attractive and admired, even though they finished behind teams who adopted harder methods.

Nothing that he saw in the World Cup finals made Greenwood change his mind. He saw fouls aplenty, but rejoiced in the flowing movement of the Dutch, the deadly finishing of the champions Argentina, the rapidly developing know-how of the Africans and the Asians.

"Look at the Italians," he said sadly after they had lost a place in the final. "Enzo Bearzot has done a marvellous job changing their attitude, but when they were a goal up at half time they fell back into old habits. If only they had the courage of their convictions and kept going forward".

England took him at his word when we came back from Argentina and his own team got down to business in the European Championship. A 4–3 victory in Denmark brought wails of concern about our defence.

Even in a 4–nil win over Northern Ireland, which sent England to Bulgaria as group leaders, the manager was criticised. This time, for his loyalty to certain players.

To a man whose approach is as dear to him as the blood that runs through his veins, such accusations matter little. After all, had not Don Revie been maligned over changing the team *too much*?

We were back to that word continuity. Greenwood knows England will achieve nothing without the confidence and understanding which only develops when players have some measure of security.

But results *do* matter, and the European Championship is something both Revie and Ramsey failed to win. How England fare in 1980 may determine whether Greenwood seeks, or is offered, an extension up to the World Cup of 1982.

Greenwood would not be human if he did not see success in Italy next summer, or better still in Spain two years later, as a natural climax to a career which has always manifested his love of the game.

Some of his happiest moments were spent pitting his tactical brain against that of other European coaches during West Ham's successful years in the Cup-winners Cup in 1965 and in 1976.

The twinkle in his eye has more to do with how to exploit space and angles in the opposing penalty area, than with how best to stop the opposition when they come into your own half.

In other words, he wants to test the pedigree of his team against brains rather than brawn. To lift the game to the intelligent, almost academic level where he has always believed it should be played.

Mind you, don't make the mistake of

Ron Greenwood in his playing days with Chelsea.

thinking Greenwood overcomplicates things when he speaks about football. He has always said it is a simple game which is sometimes made difficult by those who play it.

Hence a certain innocence about the way England played last season, because Greenwood has never been one to close up the game; he acknowledges the opposition's right to express themselves in the way he demands that right for his own players.

But beyond being a purist, a thinker, a practical man of high principle, Ron Greenwood is something else that England needs. He is an ambassador.

England may not be the football force of old, but everywhere our teams travel there is a respect and a curiosity born out of the fact that we taught the game to the world.

Justice can only be done to such a reputation if the figure at the head of England's ranks commands the respect of those who meet him.

Developing skills, learning football's fundamentals . . . these matter more to Ron Greenwood than winning cups and medals.

In that sense, Greenwood is to England what Helmut Schoen was to West Germany; what Enzo Bearzot has become to Italy; what Cesar Luis Menotti proved to be for Argentina when they became World Champions.

These are men of dignity and stature as well as having vast football knowledge and experience. They believe in old-fashioned virtues like the spirit and ethos of the game as well as exposing themselves to its fierce, modern demands.

Football in Germany, in Italy and in Argentina needed a change of image when those managers moved into the job. That is precisely the situation in which Greenwood found himself.

So what then are the reservations? Only the fact that he will still be judged, in the short term, by what England achieve on the field.

Only the fact that his benevolent attitude may mean we shall concede a few too many goals.

With his innate sense of fairness, Greenwood will not lower himself to acts of petty gamesmanship that others will employ when the competition is at its hardest. In that respect, England will always finish second when it comes to sharp practice.

We have got to hope that the wholesome qualities discussed earlier will outweigh any devious designs that others try to force on the new England. We must stand by Greenwood's belief that honesty is the best policy.

Because, whatever happens to the full England team in the next critical months, rest assured that it is no longer living in isolation.

Behind the showpiece matches in the European Championship, a structure is now emerging which, given time and licence, will guarantee a firmer and more productive family tree for English football in the future.

Ron Greenwood has built his platform. Let us hope the men he chooses, at all levels, can perform on it to his own high standards.

31

FUNSPOT - FUNSPOT - FUNSPOT - FUNSPOT - FUNSPOT - FUNSPOT

Clues across

1 John Toshack has become one in Wales
5 Top scorer for West Ham United
9 One of Brazil's greatest-ever stars
10 Rarely seen number
12 What players do at half-time
13 A Linfield, Hibernian and Sunderland Irish international in the 1960s
17 Beaten sides are often called this
18 A drink in Port Vale
19 A Sunderland player and then manager
20 Someone to look up to
23 Time . . . . . on for injury
24 Usual number of minutes played
26 Famous Yorkshire club
30 Might stand for Save Our Soccer
31 Fans packed on the terraces often look like a . . . .
32 The top division
34 Coaches show you the . . . to play
35 In cold weather a fan . . . . . up
38 You are this if in the crowd
40 By way of—your route to the ground
41 Ronnie . . . . . previous West Bromwich Albion manager and goalscorer
43 Shows keen interest
47 Holds two Bristol City records
49 Right round the pitch
50 A pools windfall?
52 Reading's . . . Park
53 Former midfield player and manager of several clubs, Jim . . . .
54 Sounds like the referee's whistle
56 Disapproving sound
58 Cyril . . . Ipswich and Wales trainer
59 You may feel this after playing
60 East London club
61 One end at Chelsea

Clues down

1 Ankle injury?
2 A little Scot?
3 Australian World Cup player 1974 and also appeared in Football League
4 Behind the goal
5 After cup draws
6 Part of the woodwork
7 An individual goal
8 Cried over losing?
11 Money to enter ground?
14 A short addition
15 Blackburn Rovers defender
16 Alex . . . . . ex-Burnley, Stoke and Irish international defender
17 Scouts are always on the look out for one
21 Brazilian World Cup star and later Peru's manager
22 Smaller crowds mean this
25 Another word for aggregate
27 Could be an Eddie
28 Healthy spot for special training
29 Travel by this to the match
31 Was in possession of, or . . . the ball
32 . . . Park, a Scottish ground
33 This name has been honoured internationally at the turn of the century in Northern Ireland
34 It ruined the 1978–79 season
36 Think of a highly-regarded player like this
37 Feeling of hunger after a match?
39 Another word for intended
40 Former Manchester United and England player, Dennis . . . .
42 Referee of the 1954 F.A. Cup Final
44 Former test cricketer who also played League football in pre-war days
45 Defenders can be . . . . . . by skilful opponents
46 Search a defensive wall for one
48 A slippery winger?
50 Coaching instructions can be shown on it
51 First Spanish winners of the European Cup
55 Unpopular decisions raise this in the crowd
56 Is in possession of, or . . . the ball
57 Feminine fan

Answers: see page 59

To play: You need a dice—or you can cut out or trace round the spinner (right) and glue it on to a piece of card, pushing a matchstick through the centre and scoring the number on which it comes to rest. You can play the game with tiddly-winks, or you can cut out or trace round the footballers below and glue these on to pieces of card. Two, three or four players can take part. And remember, every time you get a six, you win an extra go. Now you're ready to set off on the road to Wembley—Up for the Cup!

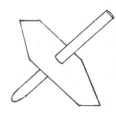

41 £250.000 striker signed- move on 2 squares	42	43	44	45
40	39	38 Manager resigns- miss a turn	37	36 Winning run- move on 3 squares
21	22	23	24	25 Winning run- move on 3 squares
20	19 Goals scored- have an extra turn!	18 Goals given away- miss a turn!	17	16
START → 1	2	3	4	5 Injury to key player- go back 3 squares!

Up for the Cup!

46 Goals given away- miss a turn!

47 Goals scored- have an extra turn!

48

49 Injury to key player- go back 3 squares!

50

35

34

33

32

31 Ground flooded- miss a turn

26

27 Losing run- wait to throw a six!

28

29

30

15

14

13 Losing run- wait to throw a six!

12

11

6

7 Goals given away- miss a turn!

8 Goals scored- have an extra turn!

9

10

Barry Davies meets soccer's great Dane

Simonsen - a giant in size six boots

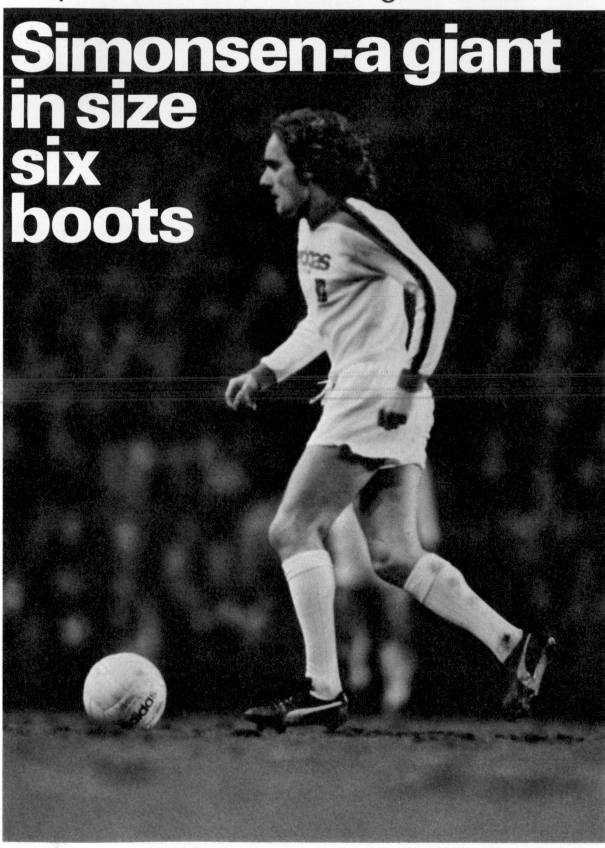

WHEN ALLAN SIMONSEN joined Borussia Moenchengladbach as a shy 20-year-old Dane, just five foot six inches tall and wearing only size six football boots, Gunther Netzer, then at the height of his power as conductor of the West German national team, asked: "What is this, a kindergarten?" Six years later, Netzer, now the general manager of Hamburg, tried desperately to find enough money to sign the object of his jibe—and failed.

Netzer's aim had been to bring together two little men who over the last two years have cast a giant shadow across Europe, Simonsen and Kevin Keegan. The dream is now Barcelona's. Having signed Simonsen on a three-year contract for a reported fee of £1·2 million at the end of last season, they would now like to see Netzer lose the services of the other mighty mouse . . .

It was in Rome on the balmy evening of May 25 1977 that Simonsen really introduced himself to a British audience. And for 15 minutes he was a most unwelcome visitor in millions of homes around the land. Intercepting a pass from Jimmy Case which caught Phil Neal coming forward, Simonsen at once cut inside the full back and unleashed a shot of such ferocity and spin that Ray Clemence was beaten before he had time for preparation.

The scoreboard in the Olympic Stadium and the captions on the television screens read Borussia Moenchengladbach 1, Liverpool 1. It was, as we know now, but a classic consolation goal for the German side on a night of glory for Bob Paisley and his team, but until Tommy Smith strode forward as an unlikely but so welcome hero it raised many a pulse rate.

The reward for Simonsen was that it clinched his selection as European Footballer of the Year ahead of the man of the match in Rome, Kevin Keegan. A year later Simonsen was supporting Keegan to succeed him. And the admiration of one for the other ("Who would not want to play in the same side as Keegan, he offers so much") reached the point when at the time of the Simonsen transfer Keegan said that he was the best player in the world.

When I passed this observation on to the very likeable Dane, he reacted with the embarrassment of a schoolboy who had just been told he was the best in the team. "It's very nice of him to say so but I don't think it is true. People say I am a star, but I don't think

Dedicated and determined, Simonsen has the skill and fitness to more than compensate for his lack of pounds and inches.

about it. Of course, I am pleased when I do well and make goals, but I do it for a team not just for me."

Remarks like that suggest a coach's dream, an outstanding individual player conscious of his responsibility; but there can be little doubt that the captaincy of a struggling Borussia side last season took a certain edge off his play.

It may, though, have longer-term benefits in preparing a quiet, introvert character for the rigours of the Spanish media. When he first came to Germany he would stay in the dressing room to avoid reporters. "As the captain, I was asked more and as I have become older I have learned that people want information about me and as they come to watch the team and help pay our wages that is their right." It is a theory currently undergoing its biggest test in Barcelona.

There are three major reasons for Simonsen's success. His own dedication, particularly in overcoming the apparent limitations of his physique, and the advice of two men . . .

"I was always going to be a footballer from

May 25 1977 . . . Simonsen scored for Borussia Moenchengladbach, but it was Kevin Keegan's Liverpool who won the European Cup.

the days my father took me to every match he played. At school I used to play in every break from lessons. Of course, there were other sports, like handball and gymnastics, but football always came first.'' And if gymnastics is the reason why he gets up far better than a man of his size is entitled to, there is no doubting his belief that his lack of pounds and inches has made him the player he is.

''I was always much smaller than anyone else and from my first day at school I must live with it. I think it is why my football is technical and why I am fast. Since I am five years it has been this way. My father was the same and I play the way he played.''

His father, Gert, played for Vejle Bokclub, one of the top clubs in Denmark, and when he was ten Simonsen followed him there. There was a moment when he almost left to join some friends who felt they would do better with a lesser club. ''But when I told my father he said I should go and put my boots away. Either I played for a top club or I didn't play at all.''

At the age of 17 he went with Vejle to a youth tournament in Dusseldorf and it was there that he met Hennes Weisweiler, the autocratic coach of Borussia Moenchengladbach. ''He wanted to sign me

then, I told him that I must first complete my studies but that I should come in two years.''

So, while learning to be a car salesman with Volkswagen at their factory in Vejle, he was available to play for Denmark in the 1972 Olympics. But he was selected only as a late replacement, even though he had scored twice on his debut in a 5–2 victory in Iceland.

The Danes did well in the competition, reaching the semi-final group, where they held Poland, the eventual winners.

The year after the Games he kept his promise to Weisweiler and began an apprenticeship in a school even harder than he expected. ''I knew it would be difficult for me, that I should have to work hard on my physique and learn to cope with man-for-man marking, but there were times when I wondered if Mr Weisweiler had a heart. Every day I was paired in training with Berti Vogts.''

He paused for a second before adding with a slightly nervous smile: ''I think it says enough. In all that time Mr Weisweiler never spoke to me. But he believes a lot in training with the ball and he's really the reason why I have become the player I am today.''

His own patience ("I knew that I had to keep at it or go back to Denmark"), the encouragement of his wife, Anetta, and the friendship of a fellow Dane, Henning Jensen, helped him to conquer his doubts and prove to Weisweiler that he deserved a place in the team. But it took 16 months. "Then things became a bit easier . . . still very hard, but we talked a little."

Simonsen's club partnership with Jensen lasted until 1976 when the Danish international centre forward was transferred to Real Madrid and now the friends find themselves at the heart of the intense and sometimes spiteful rivalry between Spain's two senior clubs, with Simonsen looking to find the same on-the-field understanding with a not dissimilar player, Hans Krankl, the Austrian World Cup star.

There is no doubt that Jensen helped influence Simonsen's decision to go to Barcelona after winning medals for three championships, two UEFA Cups and for finishing as runners-up in the European Cup. "I had heard lots of good things about Spain. My wife and I wanted to try somewhere new and we liked the sun and the mentality of people there."

Almost as an afterthought he added "and, of course there was the economic angle". But, while he lives modestly and rarely talks about money, a whole year of bargaining with Barcelona with the help of his adviser, Eigil Jensen, the secretary of Vejle, hardly suggests an innocent abroad.

He signed without knowing who his new coach would be and without fear of the more cynical tactics of Spanish football—"As a moving player I shall be more difficult to hit".

His contract runs until 1982 and he refuses to look any further than that, other than to hope that the increase in the number of finalists to 24 will give him the chance of playing in the World Cup in Spain that year. "It has always been difficult for us with our players coming from clubs all over Europe, but with our association making sure that they must now come back to play for Denmark we have our best chance. And for the first time we have a full-time professional coach."

He's Sepp Piontek, a former West German international, who has coached Werder Bremen and St Pauli and also had a spell with the Haitian national side. And if he can bring some organisation to a deal of natural talent, which is now backed by Carlsberg Breweries to the tune of £100,000 a year, perhaps Denmark will surprise a few. They will, though, need to be less profligate with scoring chances than they have been in the current European Championships.

Unlike the clubs in Common Market countries, Barcelona are not subject to a fine should they fail to grant Simonsen's release, but, with an air of calmness which borders naivety, he is quite sure the clause will be honoured.

In a way that sums up his whole approach. He has planned for his future by buying land in Denmark and hopes soon to open a factory for sports equipment. He's well aware of the standard of living he can now offer his wife and two-year-old daughter, Camilla, but says that he and Anetta have never talked about how things have changed.

He knows he has made and is making a fortune out of size six boots but this quiet young man, who would have to put sleep high on his list of off-the-field activities, is completely unspoiled by success—"I hope my friends at home would find me just the same." And when he says "my life is football and it gives me pleasure", he is not deliberately understating the case. That, quite simply, is how he sees it.

FUNSPOT - FUNSPOT - FUNSPOT - FUNSPOT - FUNSPOT - FUNSPOT

Fill in the spaces with letters which will make up the names of different football teams across the page, nine in all. But the column down in the centre also has the name of another team and you must find the correct teams across to complete the one down.

Answers: See page 59.

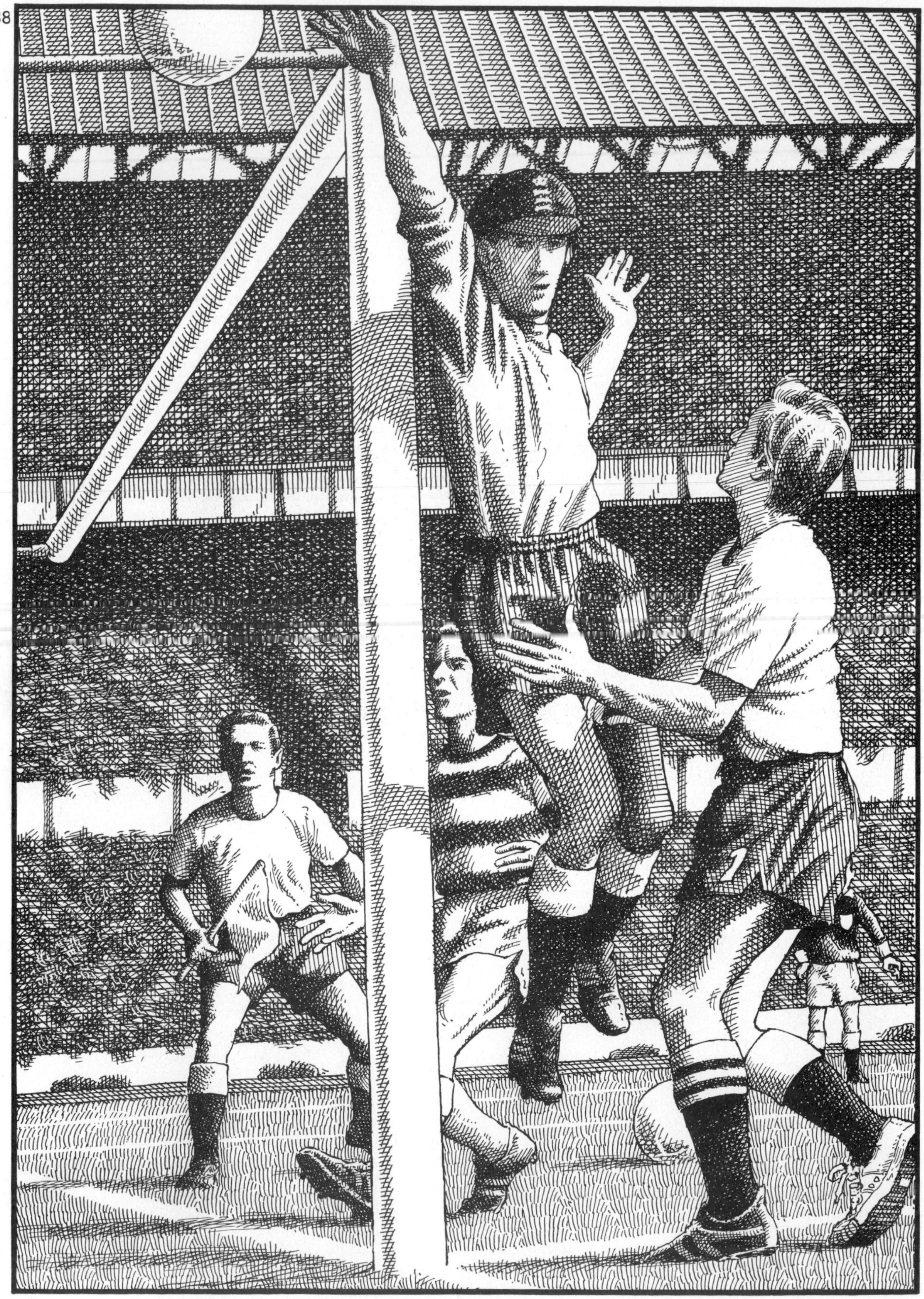

Match of the Day... always a winner!

MATCH OF THE DAY was born on August 22 1964. It arrived on the TV screens on BBC2,

presented 45 minutes of highlights from the First Division match, Liverpool v Arsenal, and was watched by an audience of 60,000.

Today its regular weekly audience is enough to fill Wembley Stadium more than 120 times and Match of the Day is respected all over the world as television's most comprehensive football programme.

It's been an exciting 15 years and, throughout, Match of the Day has been in the forefront of advances made in the techniques and technology of football coverage.

From the very start, Match of the Day used electronic cameras and recorded on to video tape. And then in 1965 it brought in zoom lenses for the first time.

In August 1966 —the year of England's World Cup triumph —came a significant change. Match of the Day switched from BBC2 to BBC1.

This was the real watershed, transforming football from a television sport into a wildly popular television subject.

This was the year, too, that saw the introduction of the slow-motion action-replay machine, which was used exclusively on Match of the Day together with an electronic camera positioned behind goal to replay

FUNSPOT - FUNSPOT - FUNSPOT

How much do you know about football? And how observant are you? Find out by studying the picture opposite. It contains 10 errors. Can you spot them? Answers on page 59.

incidents from a different angle.

In November 1967 the programme chalked up its 100th edition. And two years later—in August, when Barry Davies joined the programme's team—came the decision to transmit two matches each Saturday.

In November 1969, Match of the Day was back on BBC2 —for one match only so that a League game (Liverpool v West Ham was the match chosen) could be shown in colour. At the time, of course, BBC1 was still transmitting in black and white only.

The first Goal of the Month competition was introduced in September 1970 and was immediately established as a Match of the Day firm favourite.

John Motson joined in August 1971 and two years later the programme recruited one of the famous names in football—Jimmy Hill.

With the start of the 1977 football season, Match of the Day celebrated its 500th edition.

1978/79 Roll of Honour

League Champions:
LIVERPOOL
FA Cup:
ARSENAL
League Cup:
NOTTINGHAM FOREST
Scottish League Champions:
CELTIC
Scottish FA Cup:
RANGERS
Scottish League Cup:
RANGERS
European Cup:
NOTTINGHAM FOREST
European Cup-winners' Cup:
BARCELONA
UEFA Cup:
BORUSSIA MOENCHENGLADBACH

DAVE WATSON. Despite a lengthy career, Dave Watson has really only established himself as a first-class centre-half in recent years. He also had spells at centre-forward and was with Notts County before moving on to Rotherham United and then Sunderland. Transferred to Manchester City in the summer of 1975 for £200,000 he has made over 450 League appearances with his various senior clubs. After making his first full appearance for England in 1974 he gradually settled into regular selection and was awarded his 44th full honour against Austria in June 1979.

· HALL OF FAME · HALL OF FAME · HALL OF FAME · HALL OF FAME ·

TONY CURRIE. A midfield player who started with Watford after brief trials with Chelsea and Queen's Park Rangers, Tony Currie was transferred to Sheffield United a month after his 18th birthday in February 1968 for £26,500. In the close season of 1976 he made another move in Yorkshire when Leeds United paid £250,000 for his services. After gaining England Under-23 honours he had added 17 full appearances by June 1979. He has made well over 400 League appearances in his career and developed his all-round ability as an outstanding schemer of class.

HALL OF FAME · HALL OF FAME · HALL OF FAME · HALL OF FAME ·

DEREK JOHNSTONE made an immediate impact in the senior game in Scotland. He was only 16 when he scored the winning goal in the Scottish League Cup Final for Rangers against Celtic in October 1970. He also equalised in the Scottish Cup Final later in the season against the same opponents. Has been used by Rangers at centre-half or as a centre-forward, where he is particularly dangerous in the air. He scored both goals for Scotland in the Home International Championship in 1978 but did not get a game in the following World Cup finals in Argentina.

· HALL OF FAME · HALL OF FAME · HALL OF FAME · HALL OF FAME ·

LIAM BRADY was the Professional Footballers Association's choice as Player of the Year in 1978–79. This Dublin-born Republic of Ireland international midfield player made his debut for Arsenal early in the 1973–74 season. He completed his 150th League appearance for the club during 1977–78 and has shown himself to be a useful marksman including goals from free-kicks and penalties. He has been honoured by his country at several levels including 22 full appearances; a figure he reached against Argentina in May 1979. He has a fine range of skills.

HALL OF FAME · HALL OF FAME · HALL OF FAME · HALL OF FAME ·

Polish a skill

with Bob Wilson

EVERY WEEK in Britain alone thousands of people flock to their local football grounds. Yet on average they see only one or two goals, so just what is it that proves such an attraction?

For all but the real soccer purist, it is that unexpected moment of skill from one of those 22 players out there on the field. It might be a great save, a spectacular goal or an incredible display of ball control—and that is just what the game is all about.

For players such as Pele, Cruyff and Best these moments of magic came naturally, but others are not so fortunate.

Yet in his own way every player has something of a Pele or Cruyff in him, because we all have at least one little trick in our game which is something special.

It might be an overhead kick, a clever turn or a shot on the volley—we all love to do the spectacular, especially if we know the other

players on the field haven't the same ability.

That particular skill should be developed and practised and polished until it shines like a diamond, because that is when you will start to catch the eye in your games.

As a young goalkeeper I struggled on crosses, punches and kicking a dead ball, but I realised my greatest strength at an early stage in my career and this helped me no end in reaching the top as a player.

Diving head first at an opposing forward's feet had always been considered a courageous but rather dangerous method of goalkeeping, yet it had never bothered me and so soon I was being singled out for special attention.

I worked on every aspect of my game, but on my speciality I worked really hard, and it was for this particular method of stopping the opposition that I became well known—that's me doing it my way in the picture above.

Here I am going to talk about just five particularly eye-catching skills which you can practise. They are just five of many, but one of them may well be your speciality.

The first is probably the most spectacular of them all—the overhead or scissors kick.

1. Overhead Scissors Kick

When one talks about the scissors kick, Denis Law and Klaus Fischer are the names which most readily spring to mind—while Dennis Tueart's winning goal for Manchester City against Newcastle in the 1976 League Cup Final at Wembley serves as the perfect illustration of just how effective this skill can be when executed properly.

The expert of the overhead kick is something of a gymnast, able to take off and get his feet into the space previously occupied by his head in a split second.

The great danger with this one is the threat of injury to the back, and hard icy grounds prove especially hazardous to the overhead kicker in landing.

Practise at first by rolling on your back and perfecting the scissors movement of the legs required to obtain the full power of the kick and gradually progress to attempting it outside on a pitch, paying particular attention to your landing.

People may laugh if your attempts at the overhead kick fail, but don't be put off by this because, used to maximum effect, the scissors kick is both a spectacular and effective method of surprising the opposition.

1. Start, of course, with your back to goal and anticipate what you want to do early. Get beneath the falling ball with legs slightly bent at the knees. Defenders will assume you are going to control the ball on your chest.

2. Take off with a sharp upward thrust from the non-kicking foot, keeping your eyes on the ball and tucking into a compact and solid form.

3. This is the moment of contact achieved while travelling fast. There can be no hesitation or lack of confidence, otherwise you will be lost.

4. Kick through the ball and start to unwind from the tight position you start with. If possible, whip your shot, although if it arrives at you fast, just concentrate on your shape.

5. Take the force of the fall on your shoulders and arms.

2. Control and Volley

Skill number two is the control and volley and once again it is a potential match winner. Hans Krankl, of Austria and Barcelona, serves as a perfect example for this move, and I'm sure everybody can remember his marvellous goal against West Germany in the 1978 World Cup finals in Argentina.

The ball was aimed for Krankl from the left wing, across the face of Sepp Maier's goal, and Krankl took all the pace out of the ball with a marvellous piece of control on his foot. Before it had even hit the ground, Krankl had turned, adjusted his feet slightly into the correct position and volleyed the ball into the far side of the goal before Maier had even had a chance to move.

Control and volleying is a combined skill, calling for perfect control in the first part of the movement if the second part is even to be attempted. The control doesn't need to be simply with the foot, like Krankl, but could be with the head, chest, thigh or indeed any part of the body which can absorb the ball before volleying. In this skill there are two areas where you can fail, but you must never be afraid of failure or you will never accomplish anything within the game.

When practising the control and volley, you must be particularly alert, fully aware of what is going on around you, at what pace the ball is travelling towards you, and your exact position in relation to the goal.

At first, just practise the controlling movement with whatever part of the body you want, taking all the pace of the cross to you and turning it to just the right position for you to have a shot on the volley.

Once you have perfected that, combine the two parts of the move together, readjusting your position with enough speed to hit your shot first time and, therefore, not giving the opposing defenders any time to cover your attempt at goal.

Practise in the garden against a wall or the garage door, throwing the ball as hard as you can, taking it on your chest or foot etc., and then volleying at a specific target.

Better still, perfect the skill with somebody else throwing the ball to you, because the strength, height and angle of the cross can be varied, preparing you for any eventuality which may arise when you are attempting the chest and volley.

1. As the ball arrives decide which part of the body you are going to control it with—ie, chest thigh, foot, etc.

2. If it is the chest, make a good platform and be ready to cushion it. The principle of cushioning the ball is the same whatever area of the body you use.

3. As the ball is contacted, you must be alert and prepared to readjust your feet ready for volleying. How far you move your feet depends on how well you have controlled the ball.

4. Having made your decision to volley with the right or left foot, swing sharply and precisely and don't be scared to fail.

5. Don't be scared to go to ground if slightly off balance.

3. Drag-Back

The third skill is less spectacular than either of the first two, but is equally effective and is a skill which is used by many players throughout the country. John Robertson, Liam Brady, Clive Woods, Gordon Hill and Graham Rix are just some of the players who are experts at the drag-back—a simple but direct method of beating an opponent.

We have all seen this one operated in that moment when the winger appears to have been forced out of space by the marking full-back, yet suddenly puts his foot on top of the ball and pulls it back, wrong-footing the defender and springing clear.

You must be completely balanced to pull off the drag-back, able to turn either way so as to avoid the lunge of the defender's tackle as he attempts to stop you turning.

This is a simple skill to practise and can be carried out anywhere. It is essentially a touch practice involving the toe area of the sole of the foot and requires the minimum of space. In fact the more confined the space the better, for this makes it easier to simulate the situation the opposing defender is likely to place you in.

1. The toe area of the sole of the right foot is the vital area. You need to develop a really sensitive touch. In this starting position you invite opponents in by placing the foot on the uppermost part of the ball.

2. As the opponent makes his challenge, often diving in when tempted, stay cool, don't panic or be hurried too much, otherwise you will lose control. As for technique—pull the ball backwards towards yourself and start to turn your body in the direction you wish to move.

3. The actual drag-back and turn demands smooth and fast operation with either foot in order to leave your opponent beaten and you clear.

NB. Practise and practise the actual drag-back movement rolling the ball under your toe.

The last two skills about which I am going to talk involve turning with your back to an opponent, taking the ball past him on the way to goal.

4. Spin Turn

The first turn is executed best by two superb British footballers, Kevin Keegan and Kenny Dalglish, and involves taking the ball on the outside of the foot, controlling it and turning all in one movement.

Despite the close attentions of his marker, the man in possession finds himself with a distinct advantage because he has his back to goal.

The defender can't tackle him from behind for fear of fouling, but at the same time can't get close enough to the ball because you are in his way. He also can't see what is happening when the ball is at your feet, and, therefore, you always have the element of surprise on your side.

It is a complicated movement, which involves the controlling foot actually passing in front of the other leg. Take the ball on the outside of the foot and then whip it back across your body in a rather bow-legged action. Then is the time to turn as fast as possible without ever losing control of the ball and the defender at no time sees anything of his opponent other than his back. As with the control and volley skill you can practise this one against a wall.

1a. As the ball arrives be aware of how close your opponent is behind and if possible invite him to be tight.

1b. Be square on to the flight of the ball.

1c. Anticipate the way you intend to turn.

2. Place the controlling foot across the standing leg and keep well balanced.

3. Lean *slightly* backwards as you make contact with the outside of the foot.

4. The spin and control is achieved with a dragging action. Have your mind made up early before you attempt this skill. The flight of the incoming ball will usually make your mind up for you.

5. The Cruyff Turn

The second method of turning with the ball past a close-marking defender I will call the Johan Cruyff turn—because the Dutch master practically immortalised this trick for confounding the opposition.

It has since been copied with great effect by Trevor Francis, Brian Kidd and Clive Woods to name but three and all came about from Cruyff's displays in the 1974 World Cup Finals in West Germany when Holland were runners-up.

I have played against Cruyff eight times, and in every game he pulled off this particular turn, always successfully.

Basically the marked man feints to go one way by dipping the shoulder and then suddenly flicks the ball through his own legs and goes the other way.

This skill is probably the most satisfying of them all to accomplish—because not only is it eye-catching but it also makes the defender look a mug at the same time.

Once again the man in possession has the advantage of being able to see the ball at all times, and so any movement he makes is watched very carefully by the would-be tackler.

Therefore, the dummy to go one way is the

only chance he has of anticipating which way his opponent is going to turn, and we really cannot help but fall for the trickery and lunge completely the wrong way.

Trevor Francis is just one player who can work this particular turn, and after I saw him use it to beat the Queen's Park Rangers defence on *Match of the Day*, he told me that he had, indeed, been inspired by Cruyff.

He first discovered his knack for the Cruyff turn in a Birmingham City training session and found that he could fool defenders time and again with hardly any trouble.

1. As with the spin turn, invite and tempt your marker to come close. You have your back to the target.

2. Now comes the feint, in this case to the right. Make it sharp and realistic. Be an actor.

3a. Here comes the pivot on the standing foot at the same moment as turning the ball with the inside of the controlling foot.

3b. The ball is played sharply inside the standing foot and of course in the opposite direction to the earlier dummy.

Knock the ball far enough away from you to make it a smooth run away.

That is the real beauty of these little traits which transform a player from one of average ability to one respected and feared by opponents because of his ability to pull off the unexpected.

No matter how well known the move has become, as in Cruyff's case, the defender is still absolutely helpless to halt his opponent if he executes his particular skill properly.

Footballers have great similarities in many respects, but if you can develop just one skill which stands out and always works when attempted, then you are certain to stand out and catch the eye.

Here I have discussed just five breathtaking skills—there are lots more. Watch out for them at all times and then experiment yourself until you have found the one which you find so easy you cannot be stopped.

Then practise it until you don't even need to think about the right time to work it . . . instinct alone will tell you when the opportunity to display your skills has arisen.

KENNY DALGLISH. Transferred from Celtic to Liverpool for £440,000 in 1977, Kenny Dalglish settled immediately into the role of successor to Kevin Keegan at Anfield. He finished as top scorer in his first two seasons in England, averaging a goal every two matches in all competitions. He also scored the winning goal in the 1978 European Cup Final. The same year he overhauled Denis Law's record for Scotland when he won his 56th international honour at full level. He collected his 65th cap when he played against Norway in June 1979.

· HALL OF FAME · HALL OF FAME · HALL OF FAME · HALL OF FAME

TERRY YORATH, Cardiff-born midfield player, was introduced by Leeds United after joining them straight from his school. His senior opportunities were somewhat restricted at Elland Road by the considerable competition for places, though it did not stop him from making regular appearances for Wales. He made the switch to Coventry City shortly after the start of the 1976–77 season and became club captain. He has captained his country, too, in the last couple of seasons and earned his 48th cap when he played against Northern Ireland in May 1979.

HALL OF FAME · HALL OF FAME · HALL OF FAME · HALL OF FAME ·

CYRILLE REGIS, a tall, powerful centre-forward, was discovered playing for Hayes in non-league football and signed by West Bromwich Albion for a fee of only £5000 in the summer of 1977. He soon won a place in the senior side and from the beginning of December that year did not miss a League game, finishing as the club's second highest marksman with ten goals. Born in French Guyana, he has won international honours for the England Under-21 team and showed his ability as a thrustful spearhead of the attack in Albion's UEFA Cup venture during the 1978–79 season.

· HALL OF FAME · HALL OF FAME · HALL OF FAME · HALL OF FAME ·

PETER SHILTON. Nottingham Forest paid £270,000 for Peter Shilton from Stoke City in September 1977 and he played a leading role in the club's successful League Championship challenge. He began his career with Leicester City where he was understudy to Gordon Banks and made his debut while still an apprentice of only 16. His progress was such that City transferred Banks to Stoke and it was to the same club that Shilton moved in November 1974 for £340,000. Capped by England at schools, youth and Under-23 level, he won his 28th full honour against Austria in June 1979.

HALL OF FAME · HALL OF FAME · HALL OF FAME · HALL OF FAME ·

Tony Gubba asks

Will the MILLION POUND MAN pay off?

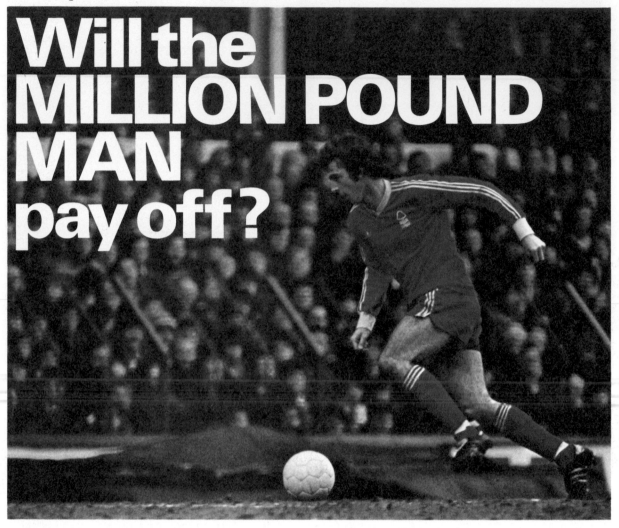

IF YOU sat Trevor Francis on the scales at the Bank of England and used gold to balance his weight you would need 2400 troy ounces of the world's most enduring currency.

One troy ounce—in the quaint jargon of the money market—is worth £114·39. So Trevor Francis, at a trim 11st 7lbs, would be worth £274,545 in his own weight of gold.

But Brian Clough, polishing his reflection in the European Cup, values Trevor at almost **four times** that amount. And who dare argue? To baptise British football's biggest-ever investment in the final of Europe's premier competition and see him score the winning goal against Swedish champions Malmo was the height of impudent brilliance.

But how much of that colossal million pound transfer fee does it pay off?

When Trevor Francis moved 50 miles from Birmingham City to Nottingham Forest in February 1979, this modest 25-year-old West Country lad became assured of a permanent place in football's history.

For as long as football books are written in the space ages to come, the name of Trevor Francis will be linked with breaking the £1 million barrier.

But what, I wonder, will the fans of Mars United and the three-legged players of Jupiter FC remember about the player whose valuation has jumped off the scales of logic.

What do we recall of Alf Common—the first four-figure footballer after his £1000 transfer from Sunderland to North-East neighbours Middlesbrough in 1905? History might question how a man could be worth £1000 in the years before the hungry protest of the Jarrow marches.

Is any man worth one million pounds—almost four times his own weight in gold—even after winning the European Cup almost single-handed?

Trevor himself admits to feeling "more than a little embarrassed" especially when strangers say "you're worth a million, can I touch you?"

"Every day I pick up a newspaper and there's something about myself" says Trevor. "I've spoken to my parents, relatives and friends and even they are getting sick of it. I never thought I'd get to this stage."

Trevor's dad, Roy, a gas board worker in Plymouth for 27 years, is in no doubt that the price was "ridiculous". Mr Francis snr has never waxed lyrical about the prodigious football talent of his eldest son. Having learned to live without excessive praise should serve Trevor Francis well under Brian Clough, from whom a grudging "not bad" is equal in value to a knighthood.

Jim Smith, the Birmingham manager who dreamed up the one million pound fee, believes that history will prove it the "snip" of all time; a bargain-basement price for nature's unique one-off assembly of the flesh and bones of Trevor Francis.

Others suspect that, like the Mad Hatter at Alice's tea-party with 10s 6d stuck in his hat, Trevor Francis has been condemned to complete his career under the questioning shadow of that emotive seven-figure sum.

It's a sobering thought that at the time of his transfer Trevor Francis had never won any football honour at club level.

Trevor's own favourite player, Scottish international Denis Law, put things neatly into perspective at the time when he said: "The lad's been a schoolboy wonder for nine years." And Brian Clough's forceful claim that "Francis needs me like an astronaut needs oxygen" was as true as it was immodest.

Certainly inherent in Forest's £1 million bid was their responsibility to provide the stage upon which the superstar could display his talents. This they did, giving Francis his first taste of European football in the Champions' Cup final in Munich. What more worthy game for Britain's first million pound player to make his European debut, score the only goal, and win his first club honour? And what more fitting occasion for Francis to loosen the millstone around his neck? The million pound investment looks gilt-edged in the glare of the European Cup.

What a difference to his eight seasons at St Andrews, most of them spent trying to keep the team in the First Division. Testament to his almost single-handed success were 25 League goals in his last full season and Birmingham's relegation just two months after his departure.

Two FA Cup semi-final appearances for the

Trevor Francis . . . has he the football skills to justify a transfer fee that makes him worth four times his weight in gold?

club ended in defeat—against Leeds in 1972, and Second Division Fulham in 1975.

From the comparative ashes of the first half of his career, Trevor Francis is now expected to rise like a phoenix and set world football ablaze. If any player is better equipped to shoulder the awesome responsibility of that £1 million millstone, then I haven't met him.

Trevor Francis is as charming, modest and level-headed a young man as any prospective mother-in-law could wish her daughter to meet. And the shy, self-effacing smile of Trevor Francis hides unexpected depths of determination.

A clue to the gritty qualities that lurk inside this introspective young man was the romantic pursuit of his pretty Welsh wife, Helen, after meeting her on holiday in Spain.

The loss of her scribbled address left Trevor with "a hairdresser's in Llanelli" as the only clue to tracking her down. His Swansea-born Birmingham colleague, Gary Emmanuel, helped collect the telephone numbers of 32 Llanelli hairdressers and Trevor had telephoned 16 of them before the elusive Helen was found, and later married.

Trevor was born in Plymouth on April 19, 1954—under the same "Aries" birth sign as Brian Clough.

But since his first day at Pennycross Primary School, when he joined the boys playing football and left them on their backsides, Trevor has never displayed the loud egotism and forceful leadership that are supposed to be the birthsign characteristics of himself and his new boss.

At the age of seven he was picked for the under-11 team. At the age of 11 he was in the under-13s. He played for Plymouth Boys and helped Devon win the South-West County Championship and reach the quarter-finals of the English Schools Trophy.

The only seed of self-doubt was sown in Trevor's make-up when he was invited for a trial with England Schoolboys and didn't get selected.

Later, when he scored a hat-trick for

Plymouth Boys against Birmingham Boys in the Midlands, and football scouts mobbed outside his door, Trevor chose to join Second Division Birmingham City because he feared "not making the grade at a First Division club".

Even today, the lasting effect of that schoolboy disappointment can be detected in Trevor's claim that youngsters in the West Country don't get a fair chance because "it's a bit of an outpost and people don't want to travel that far".

The merest suspicion of an undiscovered Trevor Francis in remotest Dartmoor would see tomorrow's roads clogged with traffic.

It's ironic that at the time when Forest, even with massive tax savings and deferred payments, were prepared to mortgage their future for the potential of Trevor Francis, that same player couldn't command a regular England international shirt.

Ever since his League debut as a 16-year-old, Trevor Francis has been described as "an England player". The headlines after he scored 15 goals in his first 15 Second Division games—including four in one match against Bolton—almost demanded his immediate inclusion in England's team alongside the old heads of Bobby Charlton, Geoff Hurst and Alan Ball.

Perhaps the Brazilians, with more romance in the soul, would dare plunge a precocious new talent on to centre-stage, but certainly not the English.

It wasn't until October 1974 that Francis, then aged 20, was named in Don Revie's England squad to face Czechoslovakia, but then forced to withdraw through injury. And it was 28 months after that, in February 1977, when Francis won his first full cap in a lightweight England team beaten 2–0 by Holland at Wembley.

Revie's admission next day that the Dutch had been better than the English at "dribbling, passing, heading and shooting" offered little constructive criticism to the embryo international.

By the date of his transfer to Nottingham, Trevor had collected a dozen English caps, including two as sub—coming on for the last eight minutes against Italy and the last six against West Germany. His two international goals were scored against Luxembourg and Hungary.

Critics could claim it's not a lot for a player who's been hailed almost as a football messiah for nine years.

Where does the career of Trevor Francis go now from the £1 million crossroads?

Kevin Keegan improved as a player after his move to Hamburg. Kenny Dalglish has confirmed at Liverpool the world class that he showed at Celtic. What can Brian Clough and Nottingham Forest make of the player, whose transfer fee was higher than those of Keegan and Dalglish added together?

Denis Law is in no doubt that Trevor will deliver the goods. "He's such a sensible boy," says Denis. "He talks common sense and he's intelligent enough to forget about that million pound fee. He's been in the limelight for nine years, but only at a poor club.

"It'll be hard to judge his success until he's played a full First Division season with Nottingham Forest, but I can't see him failing."

Trevor is a private person who likes nothing better than to relax at home listening to his collection of 250 LPs. His wife describes him as "soft-hearted". The bright lights of the city nightclubs offer no attraction. "That's not my kind of style," says Trevor. "I like going for a nice quiet beer with friends, and perhaps a bottle of wine. I enjoy that. It's important to have good friends around and I like to think that everyone's my friend.

"But you've got to be hard at certain times and when I play I play to win. There's only one result I want and that's winning. No matter what I do, I like to be the best."

The best of Trevor Francis has yet to be seen. With oxygen provided by Brian Clough, stage by courtesy of Nottingham Forest FC, this supremely talented, model professional can become one of the greatest England players of all time.

It's a prospect football awaits with eager anticipation.

FUNSPOT - FUNSPOT - FUNSPOT

Unscramble these letters, put in vowels which have been omitted and write the correct names of these teams.

SHCL	
DLRSHT	
RMXWH	
SNRGR	
NPMHSTT	
NTRV	

Answers: see page 59

For the record, don't shoot the statistician-he's doing his best says Jack Rollin, Match of the Day's football facts man

WHO? WHAT? WHEN? Ask me and I'll do my best to tell you. But, although I find trying to keep accurate football records a fascinating exercise—in fact, more of a hobby really—I can assure you it's certainly no picnic.

The chief reason for difficulties is that there is no central authority for goalscorers. The Football League and the Football Association are concerned only with the result and scoreline of competitive matches at club level so the problems have to be sorted out with the various clubs.

Most of them are keen to eliminate own goals in order to press the claims of their own players and in any case there has never been any attempt to decide what constitutes an own goal.

Some years ago, when Benny Fenton was manager of Millwall, they beat Bristol City with two goals allegedly scored by Barry Bridges. *Match of the Day* cameras confirmed that the striker had not touched either as both goals had clearly come off City defenders.

After the match I suggested to Benny that the BBC would have to start a new competition for the "Own Goal of the Month". Fortunately, he appreciated the joke. Obviously, two more goals for Bridges would have boosted his transfer market value should the club have wished to sell him at some future date. Incidentally transfer fees are not officially disclosed, either!

Soccer might take a leaf out of the book of ice hockey when trying to determine the responsibility for goalscorers. The referees—there are two—not only identify the scorers but give the assists as well, immediately after a goal is scored. And while they award no own goals in ice hockey, it would be a considerable improvement on the present soccer system if something similar could be introduced.

Goalscorers were so badly recorded at one time before the turn of the century, even ignored completely, that it was often difficult to discover the exact score of matches. It reached idiotic proportions in March 1899 when England beat Wales 4–0 or was it 4–1? The original score was reported at 4–0 but later appeared in many record books as 4–1.

Substitutes are another problem. Many sources of newspapers and annuals ignore them completely, even though they have been with us in English League football since the 1965–66 season.

It seems absurd for someone to come on to replace a player injured after a few minutes and still not be considered as part of the game. Perhaps we must blame cricket for this, where the sub is unnamed, can only field and never bats.

Bobby Charlton's 106 international appearances and 49 goals for England included one match in 1964 as a substitute against the United States of America when he came on and scored. Nobody apparently disputes that record, yet there appears to be a different standard at club level.

Arguments frequently rage in the press box at matches when it is difficult to pick out a particular goalscorer and often the presence of TV cameras can eliminate queries via the action replay. Otherwise it means an enquiry at the dressing-room door afterwards. Players will claim goals themselves and this settles other disagreements.

Occasionally a late change in a team will not be conveyed to the press and while this

Everton and Manchester City introduced numbers to the FA Cup Final in 1933; one side wore 1 to 11, the other 12 to 22.

can usually be cleared up at the time, imagine the problem when one attempts to keep records of games played thousands of miles away.

Only last season at Fulham, a League game against Cardiff City had been in progress for a few minutes when it was discovered that there were two City players wearing a No. 7 shirt. Some wag in the crowd said that it was because they were tired of being at sixes and sevens and this was a half-way improvement! Eventually the referee spotted the mistake and a No. 11 shirt was found to replace one.

Mind you, numbering of players is a rather recent innovation in terms of football life. They became compulsory in the 1939—40 season, though there had been several attempts to introduce them previously.

In 1933 the Everton and Manchester City teams wore numbers for the first time in the FA Cup Final—only they were not numbered in the usual fashion. Everton's eleven were numbered from 1 to 11 while City wore

those from 12 to 22.

Another area of confusion concerns players with the same surname playing for the same side. But when they also have the same initial it is chaotic. Before the war West Bromwich Albion had two Richardsons whose Christian name was William. So the club decided to give one a fictitious extra initial of G—which stood only for Ginger!

That was helpful but just before the war Newport County had two players with the same name with no other initials and the League referred to them as William Owen No. 1 and William Owen No. 2.

A similar problem occurred at Gateshead in the 1950s with Ken Smith No. 1 and Ken Smith No. 2. To make it worse they were both forwards and among the goals.

A couple of seasons back Tranmere Rovers had two unrelated goalkeepers named

Johnson. One was Dickie and the other David, so again there was a situation which could cause confusion.

But how about this for another problem of recent times? In November 1971 Torquay United withdrew ex-Coventry City defender Brian Hill in an FA Cup second round tie against Nuneaton Borough and replaced him with Brian Hill, an unrelated ex-Bristol City winger . . .

Another source of concern is the status of international matches. While we are accustomed in this country to full international games counting for 'caps' against similar full strength national teams from other countries, the South Americans in particular consider that every time a player wears the national jersey, it is an international appearance, regardless of the opposition.

Foreign teams present problems of a different nature. Take those of Spain and Portugal. They are likely to figure in official team sheets under their full names, not the nicknames many play under. This also involves the South Americans.

For instance, Pele would have been listed as Edson Arantes do Nascimento and while it is unlikely that he would have been mistaken for someone else the name of Arthur Antunes Coimbra might have had everyone scratching their heads. Actually that is Zico's full name.

Another practice abroad is to give players of the same name a completely different designation. Athletic Bilbao, who actually use the English spelling of the first part of their name through connections with this country in their years of formation, have had two players in recent years with the same name and they refer to them officially as Rojo I and Rojo II.

Of course 'caps' as such apply only to these islands of ours. In reality caps over here are awarded for matches against foreign teams, but in the British International Championship only one 'cap' is given for a particular series of three matches in one season.

Some Eastern European countries often field their full national team in Olympic as well as other international matches and still look upon them all as full fixtures.

After all this, there's the ever-present worry of human error creeping into everything so you'll appreciate the checking and double checking that needs to be accomplished before the state of satisfaction is reached.

But providing you mistrust everything you see in print until you are able to make reasonable checks from other sources, then, at least, the right principles are behind your records.

Who's this holding the World Cup? It's Edson Arantes do Nascimento, that's who! The world knows him better, of course, as the one and only Pele . . .

DID YOU KNOW?

● England's first substitute in a full international was Jimmy Mullen (Wolverhampton Wanderers) who took over from the injured Jackie Milburn after ten minutes of the game against Belgium in Brussels on May 18, 1950.

● Frank Sharp was with three Football League clubs in two days in February 1969. Carlisle United loaned him to Southport, recalled him on February 18 and transferred him to Cardiff City the following day.

● In the 1958–59 season Lincoln City had a centre-half called Ray Long who was 6ft 3in and an outside left named Joe Short who stood 5ft 2in.

● Chester's playing staff in 1966–67 included seven of the Jones boys: Bryn, Les, Ray, Howard, Bobby, David and Keither.

● Terry Venables, the Crystal Palace manager, was the first to win international honours for England as a player at five different levels: schoolboy, youth, amateur, under-23 and full.

● Stan Mortensen (Blackpool) made his international debut for Wales in wartime against his own country, at Wembley on September 25, 1943. He was reserve for England but when Wales lost their left-half Ivor Powell with injury it was agreed that Mortensen should take his place.

FUNSPOT ANSWERS

Page 31

Across	Down
1. Swan	1. Sprain
5. Robson	2. Wee
9. Pele	3. Alston
10. One	4. Net
12. Rest	5. Replays
13. Parke	6. Bar
17. Flop	7. Solo
18. Old	8. Wept
19. Elliott	11. Note
20. Idol	14. Add
23. Added	15. Keeley
24. Ninety	16. Elder
26. Leeds	17. Find
30. SOS	21. Didi
31. Herd	22. Less
32. First	25. Total
34. Way	27. Edwin
35. Wraps	28. Spa
38. Amid	29. Bus
40. Via	31. Had
41. Allen	32. Fir
43. Intent	33. Rea
47. Atyeo	34. Winter
49. Edge	36. Rate
50. Fortune	37. Pang
52. Elm	39. Meant
53. Iley	40. Viollet
54. Trill	42. Luty
56. Hiss	44. Edrich
58. Lea	45. Teased
59. Ache	46. Hole
60. Orient	48. Eel
61. Shed	50. Film
	51. Real
	55. Ire
	56. Has
	57. She

Page 38

1. Goalkeeper is wearing a cricket cap
2. Wrong number on defender's shorts
3. Defender is wearing odd socks
4. Defender is wearing odd footwear
5. Two balls in the picture
6. One goal post missing
7. There's no net
8. Footballer is holding linesman's flag
9. Referee is wearing white shorts
10. Incorrect line marking to base of goalpost

Page 37

Sheffield United
Grimsby Town
Port Vale
Manchester City
Rochdale
Blackpool
Brentford
AFC Bournemouth
Arsenal
Liverpool

Page 55

Chelsea

Aldershot

Wrexham

Rangers

Southampton

Everton

THE EUROPEAN

1980 is the year of the European Championship, when the survivors from two years of qualifying matches gather in Italy for the final tournament to find Europe's top national side. The last championship in 1976 was won by Czechoslovakia, who beat West Germany 5-3 on penalties after the final had ended in a 2-2 draw. On these two pages you'll find results of all the qualifying games from the seven groups that had been played at the time we went to press—plus details of the games still to be played. There's also a fill-in chart for the final tournament itself. The winners of the European Championship will be among the favourites for the World Cup in Spain in June 1982. Will the victorious nation be one of the home countries?

Group 1

Denmark	3	Eire	3
Eire	0	N. Ireland	0
Denmark	3	England	4
Denmark	2	Bulgaria	2
N. Ireland	2	Denmark	1
Eire	1	England	1
Bulgaria	0	N. Ireland	2
England	4	N. Ireland	0
Eire	2	Denmark	0
N. Ireland	2	Bulgaria	0
Bulgaria	1	Eire	0
Bulgaria	0	England	3
Denmark	4	N. Ireland	0

	P	W	D	L	F	A	Pts.
England	4	3	1	0	12	4	7
N. Ireland	6	3	1	2	6	9	7
Eire	5	1	3	1	6	5	5
Denmark	6	1	2	3	13	13	4
Bulgaria	5	1	1	3	3	9	3

12 Sep	England	Denmark	
17 Oct	Eire	Bulgaria	
17 Oct	N. Ireland	England	
31 Oct	Bulgaria	Denmark	
21 Nov	England	Bulgaria	
21 Nov	N. Ireland	Eire	
6 Feb	England	Eire	

Group 2

Norway	0	Austria	2
Belgium	1	Norway	1
Austria	3	Scotland	2
Portugal	1	Belgium	1
Scotland	3	Norway	2
Austria	1	Portugal	2
Portugal	1	Scotland	0
Belgium	1	Austria	1
Austria	0	Belgium	0
Norway	0	Portugal	1
Norway	0	Scotland	4

	P	W	D	L	F	A	Pts.
Portugal	4	3	1	0	5	2	7
Austria	5	2	2	1	7	5	6
Scotland	4	2	0	2	9	6	4
Belgium	4	0	4	0	3	3	4
Norway	5	0	1	4	3	11	1

29 Aug	Austria	Norway	
12 Sep	Norway	Belgium	
17 Oct	Belgium	Portugal	
17 Oct	Scotland	Austria	
1 Nov	Portugal	Norway	
21 Nov	Belgium	Scotland	
21 Nov	Portugal	Austria	
6 Feb	Scotland	Portugal	
28 Mar	Scotland	Belgium	

Group 3

Yugoslavia	1	Spain	2
Rumania	3	Yugoslavia	2
Spain	1	Rumania	0
Spain	5	Cyprus	0
Cyprus	0	Yugoslavia	3
Rumania	2	Spain	2
Cyprus	1	Rumania	1

	P	W	D	L	F	A	Pts.
Spain	4	3	1	0	10	3	7
Rumania	4	1	2	1	6	6	4
Yugo'via	3	1	0	2	6	5	2
Cyprus	3	0	1	2	1	9	1

10 Oct	Spain	Yugoslavia	
31 Oct	Yugoslavia	Rumania	
14 Nov	Yugoslavia	Cyprus	
18 Nov	Rumania	Cyprus	
9 Dec	Rumania	Cyprus	
9 Dec	Cyprus	Spain	

Group 4

Iceland	0	Poland	2
Holland	3	Iceland	0
E. Germany	3	Iceland	1
Switzerland	1	Holland	3
Poland	2	Switzerland	0
Holland	3	E. Germany	0
Holland	3	Switzerland	0
E. Germany	2	Poland	1
Poland	2	Holland	0
Switzerland	0	E. Germany	2
Switzerland	2	Iceland	0
Iceland	1	Switzerland	2

	P	W	D	L	F	A	Pts.
Holland	5	4	0	1	12	3	8
Poland	4	3	0	1	7	2	6
E. Germ'y	4	3	0	1	7	5	6
Switzerl'd	6	2	0	4	5	11	4
Iceland	5	0	0	5	2	12	0

5 Sep	Iceland	Holland	
12 Sep	Iceland	E. Germany	
12 Sep	Switzerland	Poland	
26 Sep	Poland	E. Germany	
10 Oct	Poland	Iceland	
13 Oct	E. Germany	Switzerland	
17 Oct	Holland	Poland	
21 Nov	E. Germany	Holland	

Group 5

France	2	Sweden	2
Sweden	1	C'vakia	3
L'bourg	1	France	3
France	3	L'bourg	0
C'vakia	2	France	0
L'bourg	0	C'vakia	3
Sweden	3	L'bourg	0

	P	W	D	L	F	A	Pts.
C'vakia	3	3	0	0	8	1	6
France	4	2	1	1	8	5	5
Sweden	3	1	1	1	6	5	3
L'bourg	4	0	0	4	1	12	0

5 Sep	Sweden	France
10 Oct	C'vakia	Sweden
23 Oct	L'bourg	Sweden
17 Nov	France	C'vakia
24 Nov	C'vakia	L'bourg

Group 6

Finland	3	Greece	0
USSR	2	Greece	0
Finland	2	Hungary	1
Hungary	2	USSR	0
Greece	8	Finland	1
Greece	4	Hungary	1
Hungary	0	Greece	0
USSR	2	Hungary	2
Finland	1	USSR	1

	P	W	D	L	F	A	Pts.
Greece	5	2	1	2	12	7	5
Finland	4	2	1	1	7	10	5
USSR	4	1	2	1	5	5	4
Hungary	5	1	2	2	6	8	4

12 Sep	Greece	USSR
17 Oct	Hungary	Finland
31 Oct	USSR	Finland

Group 7

Wales	7	Malta	0
Wales	1	Turkey	0
Malta	0	W. Germany	0
Turkey	0	W. Germany	0
Turkey	2	Malta	1
Wales	0	W. Germany	2
Malta	0	Wales	2

	P	W	D	L	F	A	Pts.
Wales	4	3	0	1	10	2	6
W. Germ'y	3	1	2	0	2	0	4
Turkey	3	1	1	1	2	2	3
Malta	4	0	1	3	1	11	1

17 Oct	W. Germany	Wales
28 Oct	Malta	Turkey
21 Nov	Turkey	Wales
22 Dec	W. Germany	Turkey
27 Feb	W. Germany	Malta

Italy, the host country, automatically qualifies for the finals. They and the seven group winners will be drawn into two groups of four. The finals will be played-off on the same pattern as the last stages of the World Cup and will be held in Italy during two weeks in June, 1980.

FIRST GROUP

SECOND GROUP

Play-off for 3rd and 4th place

FINAL

62 Fabulous Forest!

Ian Bowyer's header is on its way past the Cologne goalkeeper—and Nottingham Forest are on their way to their 1979 European Champions' Cup triumph. This spectacular goal in Cologne came in the second leg of the semi-final tie after the Germans had earned a dramatic 3—3 draw in the first leg in Nottingham. Bowyer's header was the only goal of the game and it took Forest into the final against Sweden's Malmo in Munich. There Forest won 1—0 with a goal by their million-pound footballer, Trevor Francis. Forest's win gained them their first-ever European trophy and kept the Champions' Cup in England for the third successive year, following Liverpool's successes in the previous two seasons.

Illustrations by:
Chris Ridley 3 4 5
Coloursport 6 7 7 11 12 14 15 16 18
19 20 21 22 24 27 30 36 41 48 51
53 63
Joe Wright 17
Peter Brookes 38
Popperfoto 15 58
Press Association 10 10 10 10 28
40 54
Radio Times Hulton Picture
Library 57
Sport and General 29
Sporting Pictures 25 34 35 43 49 50
Syndication International 11 13 23
39 52

Published by the British Broadcasting Corporation 35 Marylebone High Street London W1M 4AA
ISBN 0 563 17719 5
First Published 1979
© British Broadcasting Corporation 1979
Printed in England by Sir Joseph Causton & Sons Ltd, London and Eastleigh